STEM
IN OUR WORLD

GAMING TECHNOLOGY
STREAMING, VR, AND MORE

BY KIRSTY HOLMES & JOHN WOOD

Gareth Stevens
PUBLISHING

Please visit our website, www.garethstevens.com.

For a free color catalog of all our high-quality books,
call toll free 1-800-542-2595 or fax 1-877-542-2596.

Cataloging-in-Publication Data

Names: Wood, John. | Holmes, Kirsty.
Title: Gaming technology: streaming, VR, and more / John Wood and Kirsty Holmes.
Description: New York : Gareth Stevens Publishing, 2019. | Series: STEM in our world
| Includes glossary and index.
Identifiers: LCCN ISBN 9781538226391 (pbk.) | ISBN 9781538226384 (library bound) |
ISBN 9781538226407 (6 pack)
Subjects: LCSH: Internet games--Juvenile literature. | Computer games--Juvenile
literature. | Video games--Juvenile literature. | Video games--Technological
innovations--Juvenile literature.
Classification: LCC GV1469.15 W663 2019 | DDC 794.8--dc23

First Edition

Published in 2019 by
Gareth Stevens Publishing
111 East 14th Street, Suite 349
New York, NY 10003

Produced for Gareth Stevens by Booklife
Writers: John Wood & Kirsty Holmes
Editor: Holly Duhig
Designer: Ian McMullen

Printed in the United States of America

CPSIA compliance information: Batch #CS18GS: For further information, contact
Gareth Stevens, New York, New York at 1-800-542-2595.

All facts, statistics, web addresses and URLs in
this book were verified as valid and accurate at
time of writing. No responsibility for any changes
to external websites or references can be
accepted by either the author or publisher.

"All the images, videos and linked videos supplied are
the copyright of SpecialEffect. They may only be used in
the production of materials or assets that relate directly
to fundraising, awareness or promotion of SpecialEffect.
They must not be used in any circumstances where they
may be misconstrued as representing the work of any
other organisation and/or individual(s). They must not be
used by any other party or for any other purpose without
the express permission of SpecialEffect. They must not be
edited for misrepresentation, sold or lent."

CONTENTS

WORDS THAT LOOK LIKE **THIS** ARE EXPLAINED IN THE GLOSSARY ON PAGE 31.

WELCOME TO STEM SCHOOL

ATTENTION, STUDENTS. MY NAME IS PROFESSOR TESS TUBE, AND I AM YOUR TEACHER. YOU'LL BE PLEASED TO HEAR THAT TODAY'S LESSON ISN'T REALLY A LESSON AT ALL. TEACHING IS STRESSFUL, YOU KNOW, AND I NEED A BREAK. TODAY WILL BE PLAYTIME – ALL DAY!

FIDDLESTICKS! I WAS ON TRACK TO BEAT MY HIGH SCORE – I ALMOST GOT TWO POINTS! BUT ANYWAY, STEM ISN'T ALL ABOUT HIGH SCORES. STEM IS IMPORTANT IN ALL SORTS OF WAYS.

GAME OVER

SCIENCE, TECHNOLOGY, ENGINEERING, AND MATH

WHY IS STEM IMPORTANT IN ALL SORTS OF WAYS?

You can probably find STEM in almost every part of your life. Here are a few examples:

- COMPUTERS AT SCHOOL, WHICH HELP US LEARN
- TOASTERS, KETTLES, AND OVENS AT HOME, WHICH HELP US MAKE FOOD AND DRINKS
- HOSPITAL MACHINES AND MEDICINE, WHICH HELP US LIVE LONGER
- CARS, BOATS, AND PLANES, WHICH HELP US TRAVEL AROUND THE WORLD QUICKLY
- WEATHER REPORTS THAT TELL US WHAT THE WEATHER IS GOING TO BE LIKE

STEM is all about understanding and solving problems in the real world. When we have an idea of how something might work, we test it again and again to make sure it is right. Then we can create machines and **SYSTEMS** to solve the problems we have.

Sometimes we get new information, and find out that our old ideas were wrong. But that is OK – STEM subjects are all about changing your ideas based on the information you have.

NOW, STUDENTS, I SHOULD WARN YOU, I AM **VERY GOOD** AT VIDEO GAMES. BUT I PROMISE I'LL GO EASY ON YOU, AND EVEN LET YOU WIN NOW AND AGAIN, JUST TO MAKE YOU FEEL BETTER. LET'S GET OUR GAME FACES ON. SO FOCUS REEEEALLY HARD, GET YOUR THUMBS AT THE READY, AND LET'S PLAY!

STEM AND GAMING

LET'S PLAY IN THE PAST

One of the first home computer games was called Pong. Pong was a basic game which involved two players controlling "paddles" that sent a dot back and forth across the screen, like a game of ping pong. The Home Pong **CONSOLE**, by video game company Atari, connected to a television and only had one game on it.

ATARI'S HOME CONSOLE, HOME PONG, 1976

8-BIT & THE NES

In the 1980s, **8-BIT** gaming became more available. There were lots of different consoles to buy, but one of the most famous was the Nintendo Entertainment System, or NES. The NES was a small console that connected to the player's home television. It could play different games on **CARTRIDGES**, and was controlled by a handheld **PERIPHERAL** called a controller.

NES GAME CARTRIDGES

NINTENDO ENTERTAINMENT SYSTEM

THE FIRST GAME BOY

HANDHELD GAMING

As technology got better in the 1990s, game consoles got smaller. The Game Boy was a small, portable console that could play lots of games and could be taken with you anywhere you went!

One of the first home gaming consoles that could do more than just play games was the Sony PlayStation. This console used discs instead of cartridges, and could also play music and sometimes videos. Games took a big step forward, too, and games of the mid-to-late 1990s became more complicated, with huge role-playing games (RPGs) and better **GRAPHICS**.

STILL MORE TO DO

Progress is not slowing down for gaming. In fact, STEM research is making things much more fun! New technologies and inventions are being discovered every day to make playing more exciting, more realistic, and more useful!

Gaming can be fun, help us relax, and teach us new skills, like problem-solving and hand-to-eye **COORDINATION**. Gaming is also important for teaching and learning, trying out new skills, and even treating diseases. Read on to find out how…

BRRRRRRRIIII NNNNNGGGGG!

AH, THE BELL! IT LOOKS LIKE THE FUN IS ABOUT TO BEGIN. ROLL UP YOUR SLEEVES, STUDENTS. WE ARE GOING TO TAKE A LOOK AT STEM IN ACTION. LET'S TURN THE PAGE. GAME ON!

ACCESSIBLE GAMING

Most video games are played using a handheld controller with buttons and **ANALOG STICKS** to move and control the things you see on the screen. But have you ever thought about how people who can't use their hands very well play video games? Until recently, playing video games was very hard if you had a disability like this. But, thanks to some very clever STEM technology, that is all changing.

TOUCH PAD

BUTTONS

PALM GRIP

ANALOG STICK

IT TAKES ALL YOUR FINGERS AND THUMBS, AS WELL AS GOOD HAND CONTROL IN BOTH HANDS, TO USE MOST CONTROLLERS.

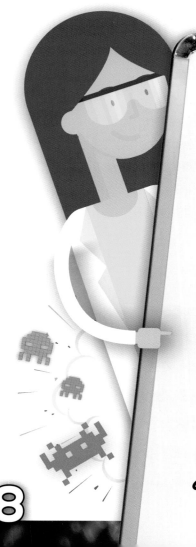

HELPING PEOPLE WITH DISABILITIES GET ACCESS TO VIDEO GAMES IS REALLY IMPORTANT WORK. FOR EXAMPLE, IF A PERSON WHO IS NOT ABLE TO PLAY A GAME OF FOOTBALL IN THE PARK CAN HAVE ACCESS TO A VIRTUAL GAME OF FOOTBALL, THEY CAN FEEL INCLUDED AND GET A SENSE OF FREEDOM THEY MIGHT NOT HAVE IN THEIR EVERYDAY LIVES. ASSISTIVE TECHNOLOGY, LIKE SPECIALLY ADAPTED SCREENS AND CONTROLLERS, HELPS TO DO THIS. SEE, I TOLD YOU STEM WAS IMPORTANT IN ALL SORTS OF WAYS!

ASSISTIVE TECHNOLOGY

Assistive technology can be designed especially for each individual person and their own special challenges and abilities. There are a few charities worldwide providing this service, usually for free. They are supported by donations and fundraising.

SPECIALEFFECT

One of the charities working in STEM to give access to all is SpecialEffect, a UK-based charity that puts fun and **INCLUSION** back into the lives of people with physical disabilities by helping them to play video games. By using technology ranging from modified joypads to eye control, they're finding a way for people to play to the very best of their abilities. By leveling the playing field, they're bringing families and friends together and having a positive impact on people's confidence and quality of life.

LARGE BUTTONS AND ADAPTED JOYSTICK.

At any one time, the charity is helping hundreds of people on an individual and ongoing basis across the UK. They also have an increasing global influence via online support to individuals and working with **HARDWARE** and **SOFTWARE** developers!

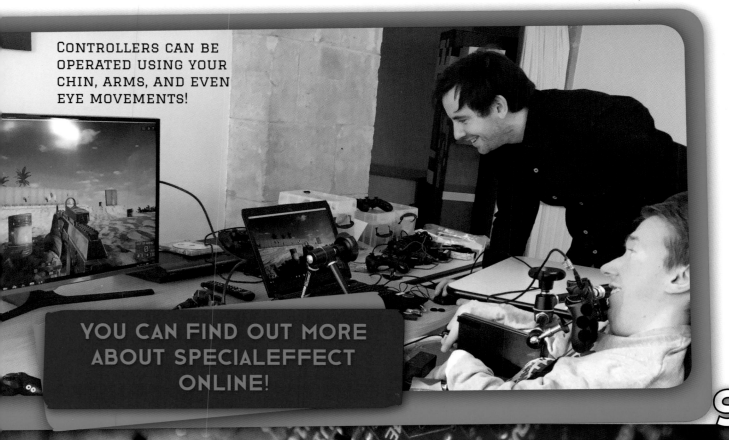

CONTROLLERS CAN BE OPERATED USING YOUR CHIN, ARMS, AND EVEN EYE MOVEMENTS!

YOU CAN FIND OUT MORE ABOUT SPECIALEFFECT ONLINE!

MOTION CAPTURE

Characters in video games have come a long way since little square plumbers jumping out of pixelated pipes!

There are two main types of motion capture, or mocap, technology. Both use a real actor's movements to create an image or *ANIMATION* in a computer game, but the way they capture these movements is different.

SUPER MARIO BROS. 2 USED SIMPLE GRAPHICS TO CREATE MARIO. HE DIDN'T LOOK VERY REALISTIC!

OPTICAL MOTION CAPTURE

In optical motion capture, the actor wears a special suit which is covered in little sensors. Sometimes these sensors are also stuck on the actor's face. Special cameras record the actors' performance, and a computer uses the information from these cameras to create a digital "skeleton" of the actor in a software program. The points on the body where the sensors are placed can then be mapped to the same points on the animated character. The animation will then move exactly how the actor did.

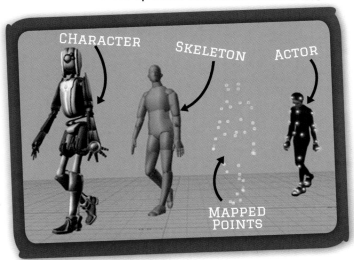

CHARACTER   SKELETON   ACTOR

MAPPED POINTS

Mocap technology can be very expensive – but as stories in video games become more and more important, this technique means that fight scenes, conversations, and characters can look very realistic.

THIS ACTOR IS WEARING A MOCAP SUIT AND PERFORMING A FIGHT FOR A VIDEO GAME. THERE ARE SENSORS ON HIS SUIT AND HIS SWORDS.

One of the most impressive uses of mocap technology in games so far is in the story-based game *Beyond: Two Souls*. Actress Ellen Page wore a mocap suit to perform as lead character Jodie. This led to a very realistic performance in the game, even though the character was animated.

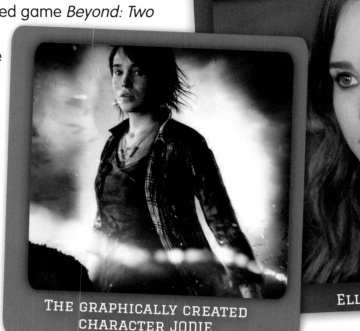

THE GRAPHICALLY CREATED CHARACTER JODIE

ELLEN PAGE

NONOPTICAL MOTION CAPTURE

Other types of mocap, known as nonoptical systems, don't use cameras to capture performances and movement. Most nonoptical systems use the movement itself, detected by lots of tiny sensors attached to the body. Each sensor measures the angle it is tilted at, the speed it is moving, and uses magnets to determine how far away it is from the other sensors. This information is sent wirelessly to a computer and is used to move an animated skeleton, just the same as the optical mocap.

I'M GOING TO BE IN A VIDEO GAME!
I WONDER WHAT CHARACTER I'LL BE?
PERHAPS A FANTASTIC SUPERHERO, FLYING
THROUGH THE AIR, SAVING EVERYONE,
DEFEATING ALL THE BAD GUYS... AND MOST
IMPORTANTLY, BEATING MY HIGH SCORE.
HANG ON... WHAT'S THAT? IS THAT... ME?

VIRTUAL REALITY

IF I'M GOING TO STOP THOSE SPACE INVADERS AND BEAT MY HIGH SCORE, I NEED TO GET INTO THE GAME. TIME TO BUST OUT SOME VERY SPECIAL TECHNOLOGY – VIRTUAL REALITY.

Virtual Reality

Virtual reality (VR) games and headsets take gaming to a whole new level. Instead of moving a character around a screen, virtual reality puts you in the game itself. In a VR game, you might be diving to the bottom of the sea, or flying through the solar system. VR takes you places you've only dreamed of, all from the comfort of your own living room.

VIRTUAL REALITY HELMETS AND HEADSETS PUT THE PLAYER IN THE HEART OF THE GAME.

VR Headsets

At the moment, to experience virtual reality, you need to wear a special headset. The headset is like a set of goggles which block out all the light around you. Most of these headsets need to be connected to a computer. Inside the goggles, motion sensors detect where your head is pointing, and tell the computer where in the virtual scene you are looking. The goggles also have small screens inside, which show you the virtual scene.

SOME HEADSETS CAN BE MADE FROM SIMPLE CARDBOARD TEMPLATES WHICH CAN BE DOWNLOADED ONLINE, AND USE A SMARTPHONE AS THE SCREEN.

What makes VR technology different from just watching on a regular flat screen is something called optical lenses. These lenses trick your eyes into thinking that what they see on the screen is real. But before we can understand how these lenses work, we need to know how our eyes work.

A lens is something that focuses light. Our eyes have built-in lenses that focus light onto special cells at the back of our eyeballs, called receptors. These receptors then translate this light into information that our brains can understand.

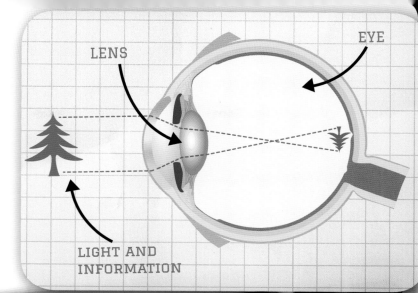

LENS

EYE

LIGHT AND INFORMATION

THESE GLASS LENSES BEND LIGHT. CAN YOU SEE THE RAINBOWS OF LIGHT ON THE SURFACE?

Light entering the eye from far away hits the eye's lens straight on. Close-up light hits the eye from an angle. When you look at something very close to you, the lenses in your eyes bend to focus the angled light and send a sharp image to your brain. The brain uses this information to help work out how far away something is. If you do this for a long time, your eyes will ache and become tired.

SPECTACLES, OR EYEGLASSES, USE LENSES TO HELP YOU FOCUS THE LIGHT ONTO YOUR RECEPTORS AND MAKE A CLEAR PICTURE FOR YOUR BRAIN. DO YOU WEAR GLASSES?

VR headsets put the screen very, very close to your eyes, so your lenses would need to bend a LOT to focus the light on your receptors. This would damage your eyes and make using a VR headset very uncomfortable.

To stop this from happening, VR headsets need to bend the light before it reaches your eyes. This way, the lens in your eye doesn't need to bend, and you don't experience eyestrain. To do this, we need two very special lenses called Fresnel lenses, and some very smart science.

LENSES   HEADSET

WHERE THE EYE
THINKS THE IMAGE IS

SCREEN

In this diagram, we can see how the Fresnel lens refocuses the light. The rocket ship shown on the screen is very close to the eye. The Fresnel lens bends the light so that it hits the eye's natural lens straight-on. The eye then focuses the light onto the receptors. Because the eye's lens knows the light is coming in straight, it thinks the rocket ship is far away. This makes the rocket ship seem real and *THREE-DIMENSIONAL*, as if it is really there.

At the moment, there are lots of different ways to use a VR headset. Most home systems involve the player sitting down wearing the headset or standing in a small area. These games usually involve you sitting down in the game, too – riding a horse in the Wild West or flying a spaceship.

Full-room systems use sensors placed around the room. These sensors can tell where you are, so you can walk around with the helmet on. The sensors tell the computer to direct you so that you don't bump into things! This system needs a big, empty room. At the moment, most people don't have this sort of space at home.

THE HTC VIVE SYSTEM ALLOWS PLAYERS TO WALK AROUND IN A VIRTUAL REALITY WORLD.

OH! OH! TAKE THAT! AND THAT! OH, THIS ISN'T HELPING AT ALL. NEVER MIND MY HIGH SCORE – HOW DO I GET OUT OF HERE? AAARGH!

SCORE = 0

HEALTH & FITNESS GAMES

PHEW! THAT WAS CLOSE! I OBVIOUSLY NEED TO WORK ON MY REFLEXES. TIME FOR A WORKOUT...

WII FIT BOARD

PHYSICAL FITNESS

When video games first became popular, people worried that sitting down and playing a game instead of riding a bike or running around the park would make everyone unhealthy. Luckily, lots of interesting STEM research has been done, and video games now exist that can actually help you stay healthy!

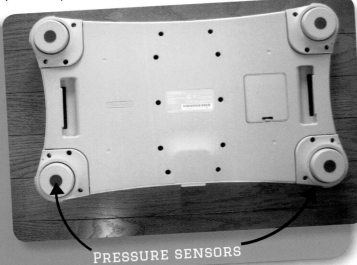

PRESSURE SENSORS

THE WII FIT WAS SO POPULAR THAT IT WAS EVEN USED BY THE US NAVY TO HELP INJURED MILITARY PERSONNEL GET BETTER.

One of the first fitness games that really took off was the Wii Fit. The Wii Fit board by Nintendo uses a small board attached to a computer. The board uses pressure sensors to detect a person's weight, and how they shift their weight around the board. The game then gives instructions for various exercises a person can do, including **AEROBICS**, yoga, and even hula-hooping! Players can see a cartoon version of themselves, called an avatar, on the screen, and the avatar makes roughly the same moves. The Wii Fit board is very small, so it can even be done in quite small spaces.

SENSING MOTION

Microsoft's Kinect device and Sony's Playstation Eye use cameras to keep track of the player, instead of pressure sensors. The game on screen would show the character moving as the player moved, and give instructions for fitness games, like boxing or running. These peripherals were designed to get people up and moving.

THE KINECT USES CAMERA SENSORS TO CREATE AN IN-GAME SKELETON OF YOUR BODY, JUST LIKE THE MOTION CAPTURE SOFTWARE.

A more recent game to get players moving has combined mobile gaming with exploring the outside world. In 2016, game studios Niantic and Nintendo worked together to create Pokémon Go, where both children and adults hunted down virtual Pokémon all over the world. Pokémon Go uses two clever pieces of technology: augmented reality and GPS.

AUGMENTED REALITY (AR)

STEM POWER:

AR uses a camera to show you a live video of your surroundings, and mapping technology to superimpose an animated graphic. Pokémon Go uses this technology to show you a Pokémon in the park or in your living room!

GLOBAL POSITIONING SYSTEM (GPS)

STEM POWER:

GPS uses satellites in space that speak to your mobile phone and show you where you are on a map. AR Pokémon can be seen on the map, and you can track your position as you hunt them down!

STREAMING

RIGHT. THE SCIENTIFIC THING TO DO WHEN FACED WITH A PROBLEM – LIKE MY HIGH SCORE – IS TO DO SOME IMPORTANT SCIENTIFIC RESEARCH. OFF TO THE INTERNET TO LOOK FOR SOME EXPERT ADVICE. THIS GUY LOOKS LIKE HE KNOWS WHAT HE'S DOING. HIS HIGH SCORE IS EVEN HIGHER THAN MINE!

ZAP

SCORE = 1,964

CRASH

BOOM

People who play games online and **BROADCAST** their gameplay for people to watch are called streamers. Video game streaming is a very popular form of online entertainment. People who like to play games might enjoy watching someone stream a game, as they can learn how to get better, or see ways to play a game differently. There are special websites dedicated to streaming games, and other sites that host videos.

GAME STREAMING CAN BE RECORDED GAMEPLAY WHICH PEOPLE CAN WATCH AGAIN AND AGAIN, OR LIVE STREAMING, WHERE THE PERSON IS PLAYING THE GAME AS THE VIEWERS WATCH AND COMMENT.

LIVE

Live

If you want to stream a video game, live or recorded, you will need some very special pieces of technology.

WEBCAM: A webcam converts light into digital pictures and sends them to your computer. This way, your fans can see your face while you play – smiling when you win and grimacing when you lose!

LIVE STREAMING IS QUICKLY BECOMING ONE OF THE FASTEST-GROWING TYPES OF SOCIAL MEDIA. VIEWERS CAN CHAT TO STREAMERS WHILE THEY PLAY, AND SOMETIMES THE STREAMERS ANSWER! SOME HAVE MILLIONS OF FANS.

HEADSET: A gaming headset lets you hear your own voice as you *NARRATE* your gameplay. It also lets you hear the sound from the game so your recording doesn't have *FEEDBACK*.

MICROPHONE: Microphones convert sound into electrical information that the computer can understand. This is how all your fans will hear your voice!

COMPUTER: Your computer will need to use a capture card to record your game. This is a smart piece of technology that records your gameplay, or *ENCODES* it, and sends the information to the website if you are live streaming.

INTERNET CONNECTION: You will need a fast Internet connection. The Internet allows your computer to connect and talk to other computers, so all your fans can tune in!

eSPORTS

eSports, also known as pro gaming, are organized multiplayer competitions where players play video games in a **TOURNAMENT** for prize money. Pro gamers play in teams or as a single player, and tournaments can be held online or in big **ARENAS** with hundreds of thousands of people watching.

ESPORTS TEAMS WILL HAVE A CAPTAIN WHO WILL GIVE COMMANDS TO THE TEAM AS THEY PLAY ONLINE.

You are too competitive.

GO TEAM TESS!

NO I'M NOT! I'M A VERY GOOD PLAYER. I JUST NEEDED A PRO GAMING TEAM TO BEAT MY HIGH SCORE FOR ME. NOW SHUT UP AND WIN!!!!!

Early rounds of eSports are usually played online, and most of the time almost anyone can join in. You will need similar technology to what you would use for streaming, and you might need some friends to be on your team.

Some tournaments have become really huge, with millions of players online. Major finals are usually played in giant arenas with a big show and lots of **SPECTATORS**. The biggest games in eSports have professional teams, whose full-time job is to play these games. At the moment, arenas use big screens to show the spectators what is going on in the game, but some new technology might be about to change all that.

THE FUTURE OF ESPORTS?

1 AR AND HOLOGRAMS

Gameplay shown on screens could be replaced with augmented reality, with animations of the gameplay in 3D on the stage as if it was happening live. A fighting game, for example, could have the human players controlling characters that could be shown as enormous AR graphics (just like Pokémon Go) or projected as **HOLOGRAMS**.

2 SMARTGLASSES

Spectators could wear smartglasses to watch. These glasses would use microcomputers and tiny cameras to show graphics, gameplay statistics, player information, and even the gameplay itself. No screens involved!

3 VIRTUAL REALITY

Both players and spectators could wear VR helmets. This would put the spectators inside the actual game, and allow them to see even tiny details as the competitors play. VR technology could also mean that people could get the arena experience without having to leave their own homes. If all the VR headsets were connected, you'd be able to see the other people inside the virtual arena and even talk to other spectators as if you were really there!

CITIZEN SCIENCE

GAMING FOR THE GREATER GOOD

A new type of online gaming might be doing more than helping people have fun. Citizen science games can use everyday people to help cure diseases, research the complicated science of human genetics, save the environment, and even discover the origins of time by searching deep space! And this isn't some clever game idea, either – it's real life!

THIS SOUNDS MUCH MORE LIKE IT! GAMES AND SCIENCE WORKING TOGETHER. I'D LOVE TO HELP IMPORTANT STEM RESEARCH TO RESOLVE THE NUMBER OF GENETIC VARIANTS OF THE FRAXINUS EXCELSIOR TREE... AND MAYBE EVEN SET A NEW HIGH SCORE! LET'S SEE...

TWO (MILLION) HEADS ARE BETTER THAN ONE

IN EYEWIRE, PLAYERS ARE GIVEN A TANGLED CUBE OF NERVES, AND HAVE TO UNWIND ALL THE DIFFERENT NERVES. IT'S A COMBINATION OF COLORING-IN AND TREASURE HUNTS. THE UNTANGLED NERVES AND *NEURONS* ARE MAPPED, HELPING SCIENTISTS UNDERSTAND THE BRAIN.

Human brains are much, much better at some things than computers are, especially at seeing patterns. Lots of science problems involve spotting patterns. If scientists and game developers work together by putting scientific problems into a colorful game with catchy music, then hundreds, thousands, or even millions of gamers will play the game. That's a lot of smart pattern-spotting heads working together. Solving problems with this many people would be much faster than using a computer. As a planet, we spend around 3 billion hours a week playing online video games. That's a lot of time that could be used in important (and fun) science!

FOLDIT

For years, scientists had been trying to work on figuring out patterns in a **PROTEIN** that caused a disease in monkeys. If they could figure out the patterns in the protein that caused the disease, they could figure out how to cure it. The computer had been trying to "fold" these proteins for 13 years. When they made the protein-folding puzzle into a game, called Foldit, the gamers solved the problem in less than three weeks.

SCIENTISTS HOPE TO USE THE INFORMATION TO CURE A SIMILAR DISEASE IN HUMANS, TOO.

OTHER GAMES

Citizen science can do lots of different things. Whale FM lets players listen to clips of whalesong and match them to other clips that sound the same. This helps scientists work out what different whale calls mean so we can, hopefully, learn what they are saying. Galaxy Zoo is a game where players look for patterns in galaxy shapes. This tells scientists all about the galaxy's history – the shapes tell them if the galaxy has collided with another galaxy or how many stars it might have. If you spot an interesting space object while playing, it might even be named after you!

THIS IS HANNY'S VOORWERP, A GIANT, GALAXY-SIZED GAS CLOUD NAMED AFTER THE GALAXY ZOO PLAYER WHO DISCOVERED IT.

23

GAMING & LEARNING

Sometimes, STEM technology developed for one thing might end up being used somewhere else. Some technology that was designed for fun has ended up being used in other ways. So next time your parents tell you that you play too many video games, tell them you're training to be a fighter pilot – or even a surgeon!

HELICOPTER FLIGHT SIMULATOR

FLIGHT SIMULATORS

FIGHTER JETS CAN FLY FASTER THAN THE SPEED OF SOUND – YOU REALLY NEED TO KNOW WHAT YOU ARE DOING BEFORE YOU TAKE OFF!

Video-gaming technology, including realistic graphics, motion control, and virtual reality, could provide a safe way for people to learn things that wouldn't be safe to explore in real life. Human beings often learn through practice, but if you are learning to fly a fighter jet, you wouldn't want to practice in one until you knew how to fly it! Simulators use wide screens and special seats that move around with the controls, so that pilots can practice taking off, flying, and landing in a very realistic way. As VR technology develops, pilots could start learning in hyper-realistic VR environments to build up their skills before taking to the skies.

COULD VR TECHNOLOGY FEATURE IN MILITARY TRAINING OF THE FUTURE?

VIRTUAL SURGERY

VR headsets, and even actual consoles like the PlayStation, can be used to teach junior doctors how to perform surgeries. This technique may even be better than learning on a real patient. Trainee doctors were less nervous when practicing on a VR model, and a study found they were less likely to make a mistake or injure a patient when they performed the surgery for real.

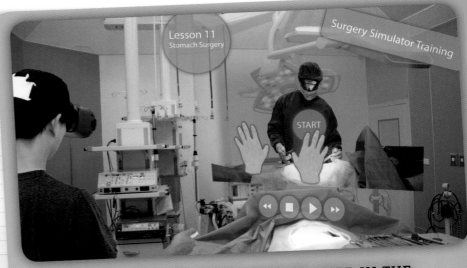

Lesson 11
Stomach Surgery

Surgery Simulator Training

START

AUGMENTED REALITY COULD ALSO BE USED IN THE FUTURE TO GUIDE SURGEONS AS THEY OPERATE.

GAMING AND LEARNING

In laparoscopic surgery, the surgeon never touches the patient. Instead, a tiny **INCISION** is made and tiny medical instruments perform the surgery. These instruments are controlled by robotic controls – basically, a joystick! A study found that surgeons who practiced video games for more than 3 hours per week were much better at laparoscopic surgery, and the better they were at the games, the better they were at the surgery!

OKAY. TIME TO GET SERIOUS. IF I'M GOING TO KICK THOSE PIXELATED EXTRA-TERRESTRIALS BACK INTO VIRTUAL OUTER SPACE, I NEED TO GET SOME SERIOUS TRAINING IN. LEARNING AND SCIENCE IS WHAT I DO BEST, AFTER ALL.

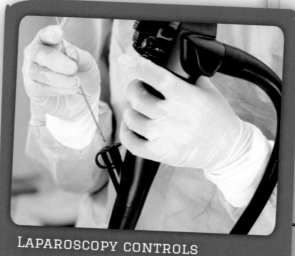

JOYSTICK GAMING CONTROLLER

LAPAROSCOPY CONTROLS

VIRTUAL REALITY THEME PARKS

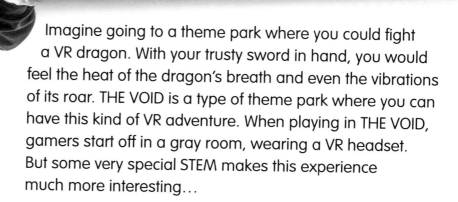

Imagine going to a theme park where you could fight a VR dragon. With your trusty sword in hand, you would feel the heat of the dragon's breath and even the vibrations of its roar. THE VOID is a type of theme park where you can have this kind of VR adventure. When playing in THE VOID, gamers start off in a gray room, wearing a VR headset. But some very special STEM makes this experience much more interesting...

HAPTIC FEEDBACK SUITS

Haptics is the name for information your body receives from its sense of touch. Many video games use haptic feedback already – if your controller vibrates in your hands, that's haptic feedback. A haptic suit is the next piece of technology after a VR helmet to really make the game feel real. If you get pushed in a game, the suit will exert a small force against your chest, sending information to the brain and telling it "someone pushed me!" The suits use electrical pulses and small vibrations to trick your body into believing what it sees in the VR headset.

HAPTIC FEEDBACK SUITS WORN IN THE VOID GIVE PHYSICAL SENSATIONS TO THE PLAYER OF TOUCH, PRESSURE, AND FORCE.

VIBRATING MICRO-MOTORS

SPECIAL EFFECTS & TRICKING THE BRAIN

VR experiences like THE VOID also add special effects in the real world, too. They use heat lamps, mist machines, fans to blow air on your skin, and props like plastic weapons and trailing strings. The more information they can send to different senses, the more your brain thinks that the VR world is reality, and the better the game becomes!

THE INFINITE HALLWAY

The last smart bit of STEM here is the Infinite Hallway. Users move around a small space, but the VR headset makes it feel as if you are walking in an endless universe. Even though the player is walking in a small circle, following a path, the VR adjusts the viewpoint a tiny bit at a time, so tiny that your eye doesn't realize what's happening. So, even though you are walking in circles, the VR headset tricks your brain so you feel as if you are walking down a never-ending straight corridor!

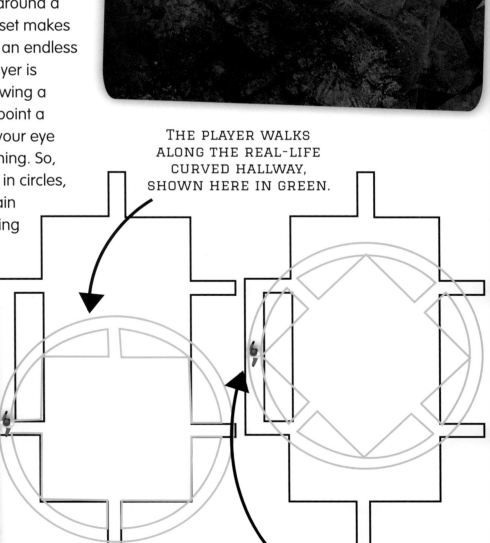

THE PLAYER WALKS ALONG THE REAL-LIFE CURVED HALLWAY, SHOWN HERE IN GREEN.

THE VR HEADSET MAKES TINY ADJUSTMENTS AND SHOWS THE PLAYER A STRAIGHT PATH, SHOWN HERE IN BLACK.

THE PLAYER IS SHOWN A VR GRAPHIC OF A STRAIGHT CORRIDOR AND BELIEVES THEY ARE WALKING IN A STRAIGHT LINE.

OOH-ERR... I'VE BEEN WEARING THIS HEADSET FOR A WHILE NOW, BUT... I DON'T FEEL VERY GOOD. IN FACT, I FEEL REALLY SICK. I THINK I NEED TO COME BACK TO THE REAL WORLD FOR A BIT AND SIT DOWN.

MOTION SICKNESS

Have you ever been traveling in a car or on a bus and suddenly, you feel sick, sleepy, and dizzy? You might even have thrown up. If you stop the car and get out, it can take a little while for this to go away. This is called motion sickness. We don't know for sure what causes it, but scientists think it has to do with a "conflict" of the senses. Your eyes see that you are moving, but the rest of the senses tell the brain that you are sitting still. Your brain then decides that you must be **HALLUCINATING**, and that this means you must have been poisoned. Your brain makes you sick, in an attempt to clear away the poison it thinks you have ingested.

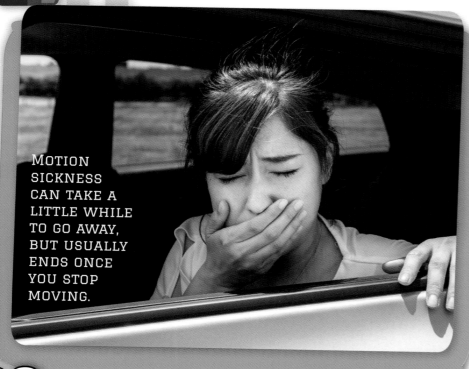

MOTION SICKNESS CAN TAKE A LITTLE WHILE TO GO AWAY, BUT USUALLY ENDS ONCE YOU STOP MOVING.

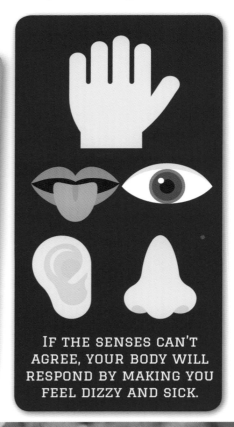

IF THE SENSES CAN'T AGREE, YOUR BODY WILL RESPOND BY MAKING YOU FEEL DIZZY AND SICK.

VIRTUAL REALITY SICKNESS

Some people have found that using VR technology makes them feel unwell. People have reported **SYMPTOMS** similar to motion sickness after using VR headsets – sometimes even after only a small amount of time in the VR world. VR sickness is slightly different from normal motion sickness, because with motion sickness you have to be actually moving, whereas VR sickness can be triggered by "visual perception of motion" – this means that your eyes see pretend movement, and you can actually be sitting still and not moving at all.

VR HEADSETS CAN CAUSE SICKNESS, DIZZINESS, SWEATING, AND FEELING **DISORIENTED**.

STEM TO THE RESCUE

At the moment, there is no good solution to this problem. Many teams of scientists are looking for a way to stop people feeling sick in a VR world. One way might be to make devices which would use small stimulators to deliver a tiny electric pulse to your head and neck, making all the senses agree. There is still much more research to be done… Could you be the scientist of the future who solves this problem?

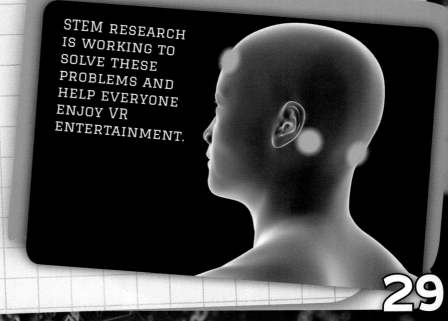

STEM RESEARCH IS WORKING TO SOLVE THESE PROBLEMS AND HELP EVERYONE ENJOY VR ENTERTAINMENT.

HOME TIME

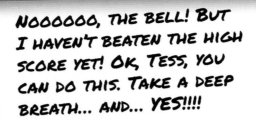

BRRRRRRR NNNNNGGGG

NOOOOOO, THE BELL! BUT I HAVEN'T BEATEN THE HIGH SCORE YET! OK, TESS, YOU CAN DO THIS. TAKE A DEEP BREATH... AND... YES!!!!

WHAT'VE WE LEARNED TODAY, STUDENTS? WE LEARNED THAT TESS IS THE BEST AT KICKING ALIEN BUTT, THAT'S WHAT! OH, AND SOME SCIENCE STUFF. ANYWAY, IF YOU LIKED STEM AND WANT TO LEARN MORE, KEEP READING...

NEW HIGH SCORE!!

Find Out More

You could see if your school has any after school STEM programs. Try talking to your teacher or your parents about how to get involved in STEM. You could also try thinking like a scientist, mathematician, or engineer yourself! STEM is all about solving problems – next time you see a problem, think about how it can be improved. You might be able to test your idea and see if it works. That is what STEM is all about.

SCORE = 2

FOLLOW THESE LINKS TO KEEP ON LEARNING ONLINE:

SCIENCE EXPERIMENTS
www.funology.com/science-experiments/

BBC SCIENCE
http://www.bbc.co.uk/education/subjects/z6svr82

SPECIALEFFECT CHARITY
https://www.specialeffect.org.uk/

CRASHCOURSE SCIENCE VIDEOS
www.youtube.com/user/crashcoursekids

Find out more about Citizen Science at
https://www.zooniverse.org/

GLOSSARY

8-BIT	simple computer graphic technology that uses 256 colors in simple pixels
ADAPTED	changed over time to suit a specific need
AEROBICS	group exercise classes based on raising heart and breathing rates
ANALOG STICKS	thumb-controlled joysticks on a video game controller, usually to control movement
ANIMATION	moving pictures created by hand-drawing or computer programs
ARENAS	a stage or enclosed area where sports events or shows are held
BROADCAST	to send a video or voice recording over television, radio, or the internet
CARTRIDGES	removable pieces of equipment that store games
CONSOLE	a home computer designed to play video games, usually via a television or built-in screen
COORDINATION	when muscles or body systems work together
DISORIENTATED	an unpleasant feeling of not being certain of one's surroundings
ENCODES	converts into code
FEEDBACK	unpleasant shrieking sound when a microphone and speaker loop a sound
GRAPHICS	computer-made visual images
HALLUCINATING	seeing, hearing, or sensing things that aren't really there
HARDWARE	the physical parts of a computer
HOLOGRAMS	a three-dimensional image formed by the interference of light beams from a laser
INCISION	a small cut made deliberately, often during surgery
INCLUSION	making sure everyone can access or be included
NARRATE	to describe events as they happen
NEURONS	a single nerve cell, including all its parts
PERIPHERAL	something you plug into a computer, such as a keyboard or controller
PROTEIN	an organic compound that performs important roles in the body
SMARTPHONE	mobile phone capable of acting like a computer
SOFTWARE	programs that make computers work
SPECTATORS	people watching a sporting event or show
SYMPTOMS	things that happen in the body suggesting that there is a disease or disorder
SYSTEMS	a group of related things that work together to produce a result
THREE-DIMENSIONAL	an object which has height, width, and depth
TOURNAMENT	an organized competition with stages and a final winner or winning team
VIRTUAL	not physically existing, but made by software to appear to exist

INDEX

PHOTO CREDITS

Front Cover – 5 – toeytoey. 6 – Joho34, JCD1981NL, Tony Webster wikicommons, Benjamin B. 7 – sv74, lassedesignen. 8 – Vyacheslav Emelyanov. 9 – SpecialEffect. 10 – Hipocrite, Joseph Gatt wikicommons, 11 – Kathy Hutchins. 12 – LightField Studios, ProstoSvet, Ljupco Smokovski. 13 – Peter Hermes Furian, RomanLebedev, Morrowind. 14 – Golubovy, jamesteohart. 15 – Colin and Sarah Northway. 16 – Juan Pinalez, Dddeco, wikicommons. 17 – Sang1938, Wachiwit, Matthew Corley. 18 – Syda Productions. 19 – Billion Photos. 20 – Gorodenkoff. 21 – Watbe, Ahmet Misirligul. 22 – Nathan Kit Kennedy wikicommons, NASA, ESA, W. Keel, Seb c'est bien. 23 – Animation Research Labs wikicommons. 24 – Sushitsky Sergey, ffly, NEstudio. 25 – Beros919, Doro Guzenda, IM_VISUALS. 26 – phloxii, Kostyantyn Ivanyshen, megula, The Void. 27 – The Void, Veronika Surovtseva. 28 – chombosan. 29 – fizkes, Dotted Yeti. 30 – Rawpixel.com. Border on all pages: rangizzz. Graph Paper – The_Pixel. Tess Tube – mayrum. Images are courtesy of Shutterstock.com. With thanks to Getty Images, Thinkstock Photo and iStockphoto.